RAISIN

The Art Of Geesekeeping: A Comprehensive Guide To Raising Geese

CHAD BRUNO

Copyright © 2023 By Chad Bruno

All Rights Reserved.

Table of Contents

Introductory..4

CHAPTER ONE...................................6

In Defense of Geese.......................6

How to Begin Raising Geese...10

CHAPTER TWO..............................18

Constructing a Geese House...18

How to Feed Geese and When to Feed Them 26

CHAPTER THREE...........................33

Medical and Animal Services.33

Upkeep and Regular Checkups 40

CHAPTER FOUR.............................48

Reproduction and Breeding...48

Education and Interaction......54

CHAPTER FIVE................................61

Geese in Several Settings 61

Fixing the Most Frequent Problems 67

Conclusion......................................74

THE END..78

Introductory

The plural form of goose, which belongs to the family Anatidae together with ducks and swans, is just geese. The honking sound of geese has become synonymous with the species, and they may be heard in many regions of the world.

• When migrating over vast distances, geese construct distinctive V-shaped flight patterns. Because of their webbed feet, they are proficient swimmers and may usually be seen in or near water. In terms of diet, geese are strictly herbivorous, subsisting on water plants, grasses, and grains.

Geese are common in folklore and literature, and they have significant symbolic or cultural meaning in various civilizations. Their coordinated flight patterns during migration have led to comparisons to ideas like collaboration and leadership.

CHAPTER ONE
In Defense of Geese

There are several compelling arguments in favor of protecting geese and other wildlife:

1. Geese contribute to ecosystem biodiversity in a natural way. Ecosystem health and stability depend on the wide variety of species on Earth, thus it's crucial that we do what we can to preserve and protect geese.

2. Goose populations are important to ecosystem health because they help keep other animal populations in check. Because of what they eat, plant numbers, especially aquatic plant populations, are kept under check. By doing so, they avoid overgrowth and protect the health of wetlands and aquatic habitats.

3. The presence and activity of geese are useful indicators of ecological health. Goose population fluctuations or behavioral changes may be an early warning indicator of pollution, habitat loss, or climate change.

4. Geese have significant cultural and recreational value in many parts of the world. They are a favorite among birdwatchers and photographers because of their gracefulness and attractiveness.

Hunting geese can be a useful source of food and protein.

5. Benefits to the Economy: Geese can be good for the economy in places where people go to observe them or hunt them, or buy and sell items linked to waterfowl.

6. Opportunities for Environmental Education and Awareness Can Be Found in the Study and Preservation of Geese and Other Wildlife. People's appreciation for biodiversity and the necessity of maintaining natural habitats can be enhanced by learning about the requirements and habits of geese.

7. Ecosystem Services: Seed dispersal and nutrient cycling are two examples of the ecosystem services provided by wildlife, including geese.

8. Research: Learning about geese and their habits can help scientists better understand animal behavior, migration patterns, and ecological relationships.

Protecting and restoring goose habitats, enforcing hunting rules, and encouraging responsible interactions with wildlife are all common components of conservation initiatives. To guarantee that future generations can reap the advantages of a diversified and vibrant natural world, it is important to take steps to preserve important species like geese.

How to Begin Raising Geese

Here are some things to think about if you want to begin working with geese, whether for observation, conservation, or any other reason:

1. Master the Geese:

• To kick things off, it's a good idea to read up on the many types of geese, as well as their habits, habitats, and migratory patterns.

This can be accomplished with the use of field guides and the internet.

2. Watch the Geese Around Town:

• To get started, look around at all the geese. You can find geese in parks, wetlands, lakes, and other natural settings.

3. Security and esteem:

• It's important to be sensitive to the geese's habitat and behavior when observing or engaging with them. Don't get too close, and don't try to talk to them.

4. Participate in Bird watching Clubs:

• Join a local bird watching group or club if you're serious about the hobby. These communities frequently plan excursions and serve as a source of information and advice.

5. Equip Yourself with Binoculars and Field Guides:

• Invest in a high-quality set of binoculars if you want to see geese from afar. Species can be identified with the aid of waterfowl and bird watching field guides.

6. Record Your Findings:

• Keep a field journal in which you can record your observations, including the time, place, and specifics of your goose sightings. This might let you track their behavior and migration patterns.

7. Join the ranks of Citizen Scientists:

• Citizen scientists are enlisted by a wide variety of groups and research projects to compile information about various species of wildlife, including geese. Find ways to aid in studies and preservation projects.

8. Go to Nature Preserves and Animal Refuges:

- Go to a sanctuary or wildlife preserve that is well-known for its geese. Tours and workshops are common attractions at these locations.

9. Aid Conservation Efforts by Doing One of These

- Give money to or join a group working to preserve goose populations and their natural environments.

10. Improvements to Habitat:

• If you have access to land near bodies of water that geese use, you may want to improve the habitat by planting natural flora and supplying fresh water. Geese may be drawn to and helped along by this.

11. Do not feed bread or other human foods to geese; instead, provide them appropriate food such broken corn, grains, or birdseed.

12. Wildlife photographers and artists often find geese to be fascinating subjects. If you're interested, look into the artistic possibilities that exist in these fields.

13. Taking into Account the Law and Good Morals:

• Learn the laws that govern geese, hunting, and protecting local and national wildlife. Follow proper protocol in interacting with any form of animals.

Always keep the geese's safety and their habitats in mind when observing or interacting with them. Contributing to the conservation of geese and learning more about these lovely birds will help you develop a greater respect for nature.

CHAPTER TWO
Constructing a Geese House

Planning ahead is essential while constructing a goose coop, goose house, or goose shelter to ensure the geese's safety and comfort. Instructions for building a goose house are as follows:

1. Planning: Think about how many geese you have or want to get before deciding on the coop's dimensions. Space requirements for geese are roughly 3–4 square feet per goose.

2. Location: Locate the coop in a safe region free from dangerous elements and predators, with easy access to fresh water and food sources.

3. Design: Construct a basic shelter with a waterproof roof, walls, and a raised or well-drained floor. Think about this:

• The roof is sloped so that precipitation runs off.

• Walls: Provide insulated or draft-free walls to guard against cold weather.

Put in some windows or a vent to let the fresh air in.

The flooring should be raised or made of easily cleaned materials like gravel or concrete.

4. Materials:

• Materials like wood, metal, or concrete are durable and can withstand the elements well. Make sure geese can safely eat them.

5. Ways In and Out:

• Install a lockable door for convenient access to the coop and to keep away predators.

6. Nesting containers: Nesting boxes with straw or hay should be provided if geese are to be raised for reproduction.

7. Places to Rest:

• While geese don't roost in the same way as chickens do, they may enjoy resting on low platforms or perches.

8. Places to Get Food and Drink:

• Allocate some room inside or right outside the coop for a feeding and watering station.

9. Safeguarding against Dangerous Animals:

• Protect your geese from foxes, raccoons, and hawks by installing wire mesh or fencing around the coop.

10. Waterproofing:

• Make sure there are no air leaks or drafts by sealing the roof and walls thoroughly.

11. Power and illumination:

• If you live in a colder climate, you may want to think about installing additional lighting or electrical outlets.

12. Convenience for Maintenance Access: Ensure that the coop is easy to clean by having a removable floor or an access door for cleaning.

13. Bedding: The floor of the coop should be covered with straw or wood shavings to provide insulation and comfort for the chickens.

14. Upkeep on a Regular Basis:

• Keep up the coop by cleaning it on a regular basis and checking it for signs of damage or deterioration.

15. Adherence to Laws and Rules:

• It's a good idea to research the zoning laws and ordinances in your area to see if keeping geese is allowed.

16. Fencing and Landscaping:

• Create a safe outdoor area for geese to roam and exercise by fencing it off and planting grass and trees.

17. Protection from Severe Storms:

• Extra protection from the elements, such as windbreaks or heat lamps in the winter, should be made available in areas that experience extreme weather.

18. Immunity from Illness:

• To stop the introduction and spread of diseases among geese, biosecurity measures must be put into place.

Researching the specific requirements and preferences of the goose species you intend to house is an absolute must before beginning construction on a goose coop. It may also be helpful to talk to local agricultural extension services or people who keep geese professionally. A healthy and happy flock of geese begins with a safe and secure coop.

How to Feed Geese and When to Feed Them

Geese need a balanced diet to thrive, so making sure they get one is important. Goose nutrition varies with age, purpose (as pets, for meat, or for egg production), and the time of year.

1. Baby Geese (0-4 Weeks):

- Goslings need starter feed designed for waterfowl, typically containing 18-20% protein.

- From the time they hatch, until they're about 4 weeks old, feed them this starter food.

Maintain a constant supply of potable water.

2. Geese at Four to Twelve Weeks of Age:

- Transitioning geese to a grower feed with a protein content of 15-16% is recommended as they reach sexual maturity.

Maintaining reliable access to clean water is especially important for their development and growth.

3. Geese of the adult age (12 weeks and up):

• A maintenance or layer feed with 14-16% protein is suitable for adult geese.

• A maintenance feed is fine for raising geese for either human consumption or as household pets.

Switching to a layer feed, which typically contains added calcium for eggshell development, is a good idea if you're raising geese for egg production.

• During the warmer months, foraging on grass and other

vegetation can make up a significant portion of their diet.

4. Free-Range Eating vs. Supplemental Food:

• Geese are natural foragers, and they enjoy grazing on grass, aquatic plants, and other vegetation. Give them access to foraging areas.

• Cracked corn, grains (like wheat or barley), vegetables (like leafy greens, carrots, and peas), and fruits (in moderation) are acceptable additions to their diet.

Bread is unhealthy for geese and should be avoided as a food source.

• Grit (small rocks or pebbles) can be provided to help geese digest their food, as they swallow it whole.

5. Changes with the Seasons:

• Feeding them more in the winter can help them keep warm and keep their weight steady. You might want to give them a little extra food and grain.

During the warmer months of spring and summer, when natural forage is plentiful, you can feed them less formulated feed and give them more time to graze.

6. True Hydration:

• Make sure geese always have access to clean water. Geese drink water to aid in digestion and to keep their feathers in good condition.

7. Layer Calcium Supplements:

• Crushed oyster shells can be a good source of calcium for geese being raised for egg production.

8. Geese should not be overfed because excess weight causes health problems. Keep an eye on their weight and health and make dietary changes as needed.

Keep in mind that geese have varying nutritional needs depending on their age, activity level, and the quality of the forage available to them. For specific recommendations on what to feed geese in your area, talk to a local poultry or waterfowl expert or agricultural extension office. Maintaining healthy, productive geese requires careful attention to their diet.

CHAPTER THREE
Medical and Animal Services

Keeping your geese in good shape is crucial to their survival. Health and veterinary care recommendations for geese are provided below.

Routine checkups:

• Make sure you inspect your geese on a regular basis for any signs of illness, injury, or strange behavior. It is critical to identify health problems early on.

Vaccinations:

• If you live in an area where diseases like avian flu are common, a vet or poultry expert should help you decide whether or not your geese need vaccinations.

Elimination of Pests:

• Internal and external parasites have been found in geese. Deworming and other treatments for external parasites, such as mites and lice, should be administered by a veterinarian.

Incubating New Birds:

• Quarantine newly introduced geese to make sure they are not infected with anything that could be passed on to the rest of the flock.

Nutrition:

• As was mentioned in a previous response, it is important to eat healthily. Proper nutrition is key to maintaining their health and immune system.

Decontaminated Water:

• Maintain a constant supply of potable water. Water that is dirty or contaminated can cause a variety of health issues.

Shelter:

• Health problems can be avoided with the help of a safe, clean, and dry place to stay. Wet air can aggravate asthma and other respiratory conditions.

Biosecurity:

• Take biosecurity precautions to lessen the spread of disease. This involves taking measures like disinfecting tools and restricting access to areas where wild waterfowl are present.

• Adequate Room and Airflow:

To avoid respiratory problems, make sure your geese have plenty of room in their coop or shelter and plenty of fresh airflow.

Regulating the Temperature:

• Geese can be easily chilled by wind and snow. In extreme cold, heat lamps or other heat sources should be provided.

Watching People's Actions

• Observe the geese's actions closely. Alterations in one's usual diet, level of physical activity, or social behavior may point to an underlying health issue.

• Know how to administer simple first aid to geese. Understanding how to treat common ailments can speed up a person's healing process.

• Connect with a veterinarian who has experience treating waterfowl or who specializes in avian medicine. They are qualified to offer assistance and guidance.

Maintaining Records:

• Keep track of your geese's medical history, including vaccinations and any treatments they've received. This can help track their health history and make informed decisions.

Euthanasia:

• Discuss the option of euthanasia with your veterinarian if your pet is terminally ill or in extreme pain.

Disease Education:

• Know the signs and symptoms of botulism, avian influenza, and respiratory infections; these are just a few of the common diseases that can affect geese.

The health of your geese depends on your prompt attention to any signs of illness or injury. Providing the best care for your flock is facilitated by regular veterinary checkups and a solid comprehension of their needs and behaviors.

Upkeep and Regular Checkups

Your geese will thrive or perish depending on how well you care for them every day. Here are some of the most important things to do each day when taking care of geese:

1. Providing Food and Water:

• Maintain a constant supply of food and drink. Make sure the water is safe to drink by checking that the containers are clean.

2. Verify the Presence of Illness or Injury:

• Keep an eye out for sick, injured, or otherwise unusual behavior in your geese. Timely intervention depends on early detection.

3. Spacious, Spotless Housing:

• Sweep the goose enclosure, be it an indoor coop or an outdoor pen. Keep the area clean by regularly removing waste, used bedding, and other debris.

4. Ventilation:

• Make sure there is enough ventilation in the coop or shelter to keep the air fresh. Inadequate ventilation can lead to a variety of respiratory problems.

5. Tracking the Temperature:

• Keep an eye on the temperature inside the shelter and make any necessary adjustments when severe weather strikes, such as turning on heat lamps when it's cold outside.

6. Egg Gathering:

• If you have laying geese, collect eggs daily to prevent them from becoming soiled or damaged.

7. Interaction with Others:

Time with the geese is time well spent. Having fun together can help them relax and get used to you.

8. Foraging As A Form Of Exercise

• Give your geese plenty of time to roam and feed. Give them a place to run around in safety and encourage them to get some exercise.

9. Grooming:

• Remove any foreign objects, such as feathers, from their beaks or eyes.

10. Safety from Predators:

• Check the enclosure and fencing for any holes or damage that could let predators into the pen with the geese.

11. Make sure the coop or shelter is safe from the elements and predators.

12. Watching How People Act:

• Keep an eye out for aggression, social conflicts, or strange vocalizations as these could be signs of trouble within the flock.

13. Algae growth can be avoided and a steady supply of clean water can be maintained if water containers are regularly cleaned and refilled.

14. Vitamins and Minerals:

• If your vet suggests it, give them dietary supplements like calcium for layer chickens.

15. Maintaining Records:

• Document your actions and observations every day. You can use this data to monitor your geese's well-being and habits.

16. Precautions for Safety

• Keep your geese away from any poisonous plants or unstable structures that could harm them.

17. Biosecurity:

• Take biosecurity precautions to lessen the spread of disease. Keep your distance from wild waterfowl and other possible disease transmitters.

18. Tenacity and Scavenging:

• Provide grit (small rocks or pebbles) for your geese so that they can digest their food and go on foraging expeditions.

Depending on the size of your flock, the time of year, and your breeding objectives, your routine care and upkeep of your geese may change. Keeping your geese healthy and happy requires regular, meticulous care.

CHAPTER FOUR
Reproduction and Breeding

Understanding the natural behaviors of geese is essential for successful breeding and reproduction. The following are the most important factors to think about when raising geese:

1. Breeding Stock Selection:

• Choose healthy, mature geese for breeding. Find people who have the right genetics and personality.

2. Goose Mating:

• Geese tend to be monogamous and stay with the same partner for life. For breeding purposes, a male gander and female goose are required. You can introduce them to each other when they are around one year old.

3. Using a Nest Box vs.

• Make sure geese have safe places to nest, like nesting boxes, to raise their young. Straw or hay should be used to line them and they should be dry and clean.

4. Laying an Egg:

• Geese are primarily a springtime nesting species. It's important to get the eggs every day so they don't get dirty or broken.

5. Incubation:

• Geese can incubate their eggs, but an incubator is also an option. The eggs hatch after an incubation period of 28-34 days, depending on the type of goose.

6. Brooding:

• Goslings need to be kept warm and safe after they hatch. It is recommended to provide a brooder with a heat lamp or alternative heating method. For the first week, keep the brooder at 95 degrees Fahrenheit (35 degrees Celsius), and then gradually lower the temperature until the birds are fully feathered.

7. Laying Goose Nutrition:

• Eggshell strength can be ensured by feeding laying geese a diet rich in calcium.

8. Gosling safety:

• Young geese are easily preyed upon and should be shielded from the elements and other dangers. A secure nesting area is required.

9. Interaction with Others:

• Spend time with goslings to help socialize them. Use a gentle touch to earn their confidence.

10. Segregating the Sexes: - If you decide you no longer want to breed, you can do so by keeping the males and females apart.

11. Genetic Diversity: - Avoid breeding closely related geese to maintain genetic diversity and reduce the risk of genetic abnormalities.

12. Ensure that both adult geese and goslings get the veterinary care they need. Keep an eye out for any symptoms of illness, and administer any necessary vaccinations.

13. Keeping Good Records: Be sure to document when you breed your birds, how many eggs you get, how many hatch, and whether or not there are any problems. Future breeding efforts can benefit from this data.

14. Ethical Considerations: - If you are unable to find good homes for goslings, you will have to deal with the ethical implications of breeding geese.

15. Legal Requirements: - If you plan to sell or trade goslings or adult birds, you should research local and national regulations concerning the breeding and sale of geese.

Taking part in the rewarding hobby of goose breeding requires dedication to the birds' health and well-being. Raising goslings and overseeing a breeding program is a lot of work, and it's important to be ready for the challenges that lie ahead. Consulting with experienced goose breeders or avian veterinarians can provide valuable guidance in your breeding efforts.

Education and Interaction

Geese require a lot of time and effort to socialize and train so that they are well-behaved and used to being around people. Instructions on how to socialize and train geese are provided below.

1. Get a Head Start:

• Goslings are the ideal time to begin training and socializing geese. At this point, they are more open to communicating with humans.

2. Time Spent With Them

• Spend time with your geese on a consistent basis. Be as close to them as possible by sitting or standing.

3. Tender Care:

• Goslings should be handled with extreme caution. As a result, there is less distrust and anxiety around people.

4. Feeding by Hand:

• If you want them to have a good experience whenever you're around, you should feed them from your hand. Don't be afraid to use healthy foods as rewards.

5. Methods That Are Calm And Gentle:

• Move slowly and calmly around geese. They are easily startled by quick movements or loud noises.

6. Keep your distance:

• Respect their need for privacy. Don't force them into an uncomfortable situation by squeezing them in a corner.

7. Get into a Schedule:

• Geese are receptive to established habits. They may feel more at ease if you feed them at regular intervals and treat them in the same way every day.

8. Please Wait:

• Geese may take some time to get used to humans. They may need some time to warm up to you before they can trust you.

9. Get to Know Other Geese:

• If you have more than one goose, make sure they get along. Positive social habits can form as a result.

10. To communicate with your geese, use soft, comforting vocal cues. They can learn to recognize you simply by the sound of your voice.

11. Expose them to novel settings, people, and experiences gradually. This has the potential to lessen worries and increase flexibility.

12. Praise and rewards should be given when your geese exhibit desirable behaviors such as coming close to you or interacting with you without fear.

13. Do not use aggressive or forceful methods, as this can cause geese to become fearful and hostile.

14. Boundaries and rules for interaction should be established. If you give geese too much food or attention, they may become spoiled.

15. Be Aware of Hormonal Changes: Geese can become more territorial and aggressive during breeding season. It's important to exercise caution now.

Geese are more versatile and fun to work with if they have been properly socialized and trained. While some geese may be more open to human interaction than others, keep in mind that each bird has its own unique personality and temperament. Building a strong rapport with your geese requires patience and an appreciation for their unique requirements.

CHAPTER FIVE
Geese in Several Settings

Geese are highly adaptable birds that can thrive in a wide range of ecosystems. Their malleability helps explain their widespread distribution. Locations where geese are commonly seen include the following:

1. Habitats in Fresh Water:

• Goose populations tend to congregate near bodies of fresh water such as lakes, ponds, rivers, and marshes. Food sources such as aquatic plants, algae, and small invertebrates are plentiful in these environments.

2. During certain times of the year, you can spot migratory goose species along the coast. Seagrasses and other vegetation in estuaries and coastal wetlands are their primary food source.

3. Grasslands:

• Geese are frequently spotted in grasslands and meadows due to their grazing habits. They feed on a wide range of grasses, sedges, and other plants native to these regions.

4. Places in the City and the Suburbs:

• Canada Geese, in particular, are well-suited to life in the city or the suburbs. They frequent grassy areas like parks and golf courses, where they can eat and drink freely.

5. Farmland:

• During the fall and winter months, geese can be seen foraging in fields in agricultural areas, where they feed on harvested grain crops.

6. Tundra:

• During the summer months, the Arctic tundra is home to nesting Snow Geese and other goose species. Tundra regions are open and free of obstructions, making them ideal for nesting and foraging.

7. Deserts:

• Oases in the desert and wetland areas are home to rare goose species. They frequently use these areas as rest stops on their migrations.

8. High Mountains:

• Geese inhabit the higher altitudes near lakes and rivers in mountainous regions like the Rockies and the Himalayas. In order to survive the winter, they might descend to lower altitudes.

9. Tropical Rain Forests

• Geese can also inhabit temperate forests where they find water sources like ponds and streams. In these environments, they may feed on various aquatic plants and insects.

10. Mangroves:

• You can spot geese of various species in mangrove ecosystems, particularly along coastlines where mangrove forests are abundant. They subsist on the plants and aquatic insects native to these regions.

11. Lakes in the Alps:

• During their migration, geese may rest at alpine lakes in mountainous regions. There is potable water and comfortable places to rest in these regions.

Geese are highly mobile, and their seasonal distribution can vary depending on the location. They are a hardy and varied group of waterfowl because of their ability to thrive in a variety of environments and feed themselves from a wide variety of resources. However, human activities and environmental changes may pose threats to certain goose species and lead to the loss of their habitat. Protecting these birds across ecosystems requires significant conservation efforts.

Fixing the Most Frequent Problems

Goose raising is a worthwhile hobby, but just like with other livestock or pets, it's not without its challenges. Some common issues that arise when raising geese, and how to fix them, are outlined below.

1. Physical Illnesses:

• Lethargy, loss of appetite, abnormal feces, or respiratory issues are all signs of illness in geese; if you notice any of these, see a veterinarian who specializes in avian care for a diagnosis and treatment plan.

2. Predators:

• Secure Housing: Protect your geese from predators like foxes, raccoons, and birds of prey by ensuring that their housing or outdoor enclosures are secure. Construct a sturdy enclosure and keep them inside it overnight.

3. Aggression:

• Geese can be aggressive during mating season or if they feel threatened, so it's important to understand their behavior. Keep your distance and don't get too close. It may be necessary to isolate violent people.

4. Noise:

• **Noise Control**: Geese can be loud, especially during breeding season. Think about where you live and if there are noise ordinances in place to control the noise that farm animals make.

5. Problems with Nesting:

• If your geese aren't successfully nesting, it could be because they don't have access to appropriate nesting boxes or sheltered areas.

Proper nesting conditions can improve reproductive success.

6. Intercourse that is not wanted:

• To avoid unwanted mating behavior during the breeding season, it is recommended to keep males and females apart.

7. Animal Socialization:

• Adding new geese to an existing flock should be done gradually to lessen stress and aggression. Keep an eye on the situation and be ready to intervene by separating the people if necessary.

8. Problems with Diet:

• If your geese don't seem to be getting enough to eat, you may want to make sure they have a well-rounded diet. Make sure they have access to clean water and give them healthy food, including any supplements they might need.

9. Insects and other pests:

• Prevention entails keeping a close eye out for external parasites (such as mites and lice) on your geese and acting swiftly to treat any problems you find. Take measures to eliminate pests from their living environment.

10. Maintain thorough records of your geese's movements, health, and habits as part of your flock management. This can help you identify patterns and address issues.

11. If your geese lay eggs, you should safeguard the nest and the eggs from harm or predators. It's important to get the eggs every day so they don't get dirty or cracked.

12. Temperature and precipitation patterns shift throughout the year, so plan accordingly. Make changes to your management practices so that people have somewhere safe and warm to go when the weather gets bad.

13. Consult a veterinarian who specializes in waterfowl or avian care for advice on how to treat any problems your birds may be having.

14. Comply with all zoning and animal control ordinances in your area pertaining to the raising of geese and other livestock.

Keep in mind that you may be dealing with a one-of-a-kind situation, so it's important to keep an eye on things and make sure your geese are getting the care they need. Expert consultation and the use of professionals' advice when problems arise can be extremely helpful.

Conclusion

Whether your motivation for raising geese is for company, food, a source of eggs, or conservation, you're sure to enjoy the experience. Although geese are resilient and adaptable birds, they still need human companionship and a deep understanding of their needs in order to thrive. The care, feeding, breeding, training, and common problems encountered when raising geese have all been discussed at length in this guide.

What you should remember most from this manual is:

The health and happiness of your geese depend on your ability to give them the shelter, food, and medical attention they need.

• Geese are highly adaptable and can be raised anywhere, from urban areas to coastal regions and even on farmland.

• Understanding the geese's natural behaviors is essential for successful breeding and socialization.

A good rapport with your geese is possible with proper training and socialization.

Responsible goose care includes keeping an eye out for and fixing common problems like illness, aggression, and pests.

It's important to treat geese as individuals with their own unique personalities and care requirements. Keeping your geese healthy and happy requires vigilant monitoring and preventative care.

If you're new to goose farming, it's important to learn as much as you can from seasoned breeders, avian veterinarians, and the latest research and developments in the field. With the right preparation and effort, you can take pleasure in the company of these remarkable birds, aid in their preservation, and reap the nutritional benefits of their eggs and meat.

THE END

Printed in Great Britain
by Amazon